P9-DBT-157

No Backbone!
The World of Invertebrates

Hairy Tarantulas

by Kathryn Camisa

Consultant: Brian V. Brown
Curator, Entomology Section
Natural History Museum of Los Angeles County

BEARPORT
PUBLISHING

NEW YORK, NEW YORK

Credits

Cover, © Allen Blake Sheldon/Animals Animals-Earth Scenes; 4-5, © Allen Blake Sheldon/Animals Animals-Earth Scenes; 7, © Andy Teare/ardea.com; 8T, © Adrian Hepworth/NHPA; 8B, © Jorg & Petra Wegner/Animals Animals-Earth Scenes; 9, © Mark Moffett/Minden Pictures; 11, © P. Wegner/Arco Images/Peter Arnold Inc.; 13, © John Mitchell/Photo Researchers, Inc.; 14, © James Carmichael Jr./NHPA; 15, © BIOS-Auteurs Cavignaux Bruno/Peter Arnold Inc.; 16, © Pascal Goetgheluck/ardea.com; 17, © Mark Moffett/Minden Pictures/Getty Images; 18, © Robert & Linda Mitchell; 19, © Francesco Tomasinelli/Photo Researchers, Inc.; 20, © Pascal Goetgheluck/ardea.com; 21, © Naude/Shutterstock; 22TL, © Troy Bartlett/Alamy; 22TR, © Bryan Reynolds/PHOTOTAKE Inc./Alamy; 22B, © Marshal Hedin; 23TL, © Jim Wehtje/Photodisc Green/Getty Images; 23TR, © Robert & Linda Mitchell; 23BL, © John Bell/Shutterstock; 23BR, © John Bell/Shutterstock.

Publisher: Kenn Goin
Editorial Director: Adam Siegel
Creative Director: Spencer Brinker
Design: Dawn Beard Creative
Photo Researcher: James O'Connor

Library of Congress Cataloging-in-Publication Data

Camisa, Kathryn.
 Hairy tarantulas / by Kathryn Camisa.
    p. cm. — (No backbone! The world of Invertebrates)
 Includes bibliographical references and index.
 ISBN-13: 978-1-59716-704-8 (library binding)
 ISBN-10: 1-59716-704-5 (library binding)
 1. Tarantulas—Juvenile literature. I. Title.

QL458.42.T5C36 2009
595.4'4—dc22

                                2008012106

For more information, write to Bearport Publishing Company, Inc., 101 Fifth Avenue, Suite 6R, New York, New York 10003. Printed in the United States of America.

10 9 8 7 6 5 4 3 2

Contents

Very Hairy, Not So Scary

Tarantulas are some of the hairiest—and biggest—**spiders** in the world.

Many people think they are also the scariest of spiders.

Yet tarantulas are not very dangerous.

They rarely bite people.

In fact, a tarantula would probably run away and hide if a person came near.

There are about 900 kinds of tarantulas. They live in deserts, rain forests, and other warm places in many parts of the world.

5

Big Bodies

Many kinds of tarantulas are very large.

One kind—the goliath birdeater tarantula—is the world's largest spider.

With its legs spread out, this tarantula is about 11 inches (28 cm) across—the same as a dinner plate!

The smallest tarantulas are about 1.5 inches (4 cm) across.

Tarantulas and all other kinds of spiders have eight legs.

Home Sweet Home

Most tarantulas dig holes in the ground, called burrows, to use as homes.

They line the entrance to their burrows with silk to keep the walls from caving in.

Some kinds of tarantulas live in trees or on other plants.

They make silk tubes to use as homes.

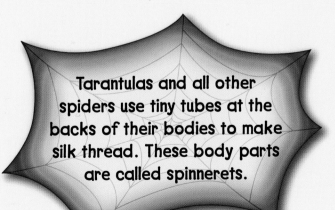

Tarantulas and all other spiders use tiny tubes at the backs of their bodies to make silk thread. These body parts are called spinnerets.

burrow

spinnerets

silk tube

Time to Hunt

Tarantulas spend most of their time hiding in their homes.

They come out only at night to hunt.

A tarantula quietly hides and waits for an insect to come close.

Then it pounces and bites its victim with its sharp **fangs**.

Tarantulas have eight eyes, but they don't see well. The hairs on their bodies feel the air move and help them know when an insect is coming near.

fangs

grasshopper

Big Appetites

Most tarantulas eat insects such as cockroaches, grasshoppers, and crickets.

They don't have teeth to chew their food, though.

Instead, tarantulas use their fangs to shoot poison into an insect to keep it from moving.

They also spit juices from their stomach onto their victim.

These juices turn the insect's soft insides into a gooey liquid that the tarantula sucks up.

Goliath birdeater tarantulas and other very large tarantulas sometimes eat small mice and baby birds.

12

bird

goliath birdeater
tarantula

13

Standing Up to Enemies

Birds, snakes, lizards, and other animals hunt tarantulas for food.

When a tarantula meets one of these enemies, it tries to defend itself.

Often it stands up on its rear legs and shows its fangs.

If the enemy doesn't back down, the tarantula will try to bite it.

The colors of many tarantulas help them stay safe. Their brown or black bodies blend in with the ground and help them hide from enemies.

A Secret Weapon

Standing tall and biting aren't a tarantula's only ways of defending itself.

The big spiders also have a secret weapon—their hair.

When frightened, a tarantula can use its legs to rub hair off its body.

The hairs fly into the air, stinging and hurting the spider's enemy.

shooting hairs

After shooting hairs at an enemy, a tarantula is sometimes left with a bald spot on its body.

Little Tarantulas

Tarantulas, like all spiders, hatch from eggs.

A female tarantula lays her eggs in her home—either her burrow or her silk tube in a tree.

She wraps the eggs in a silk bag that she makes, called an **egg sac**.

The mother tarantula stays close and protects her egg sac.

Baby tarantulas, called spiderlings, hatch from their eggs while they are still inside the sac.

egg sac

Female tarantulas can lay from 500 to 1,000 eggs inside one egg sac.

spiderlings

Big and Hairy

After hatching, spiderlings leave the egg sac.

As each one grows, it sheds its hard outer covering—called an exoskeleton—and grows a new one.

This change is called molting.

A growing tarantula molts many times.

With each molt, it becomes more and more like an adult—big, hairy, and ready to hunt.

old exoskeleton

tarantula

Tarantulas live longer than any other spider. Males live 1 to 2 years. Females can live up to 20 years.

A World of Invertebrates

An animal that has a skeleton with a **backbone** inside its body is a *vertebrate* (VUR-tuh-brit). Mammals, birds, fish, reptiles, and amphibians are all vertebrates.

An animal that does not have a skeleton with a backbone inside its body is an *invertebrate* (in-VUR-tuh-brit). More than 95 percent of all kinds of animals on Earth are invertebrates.

Some invertebrates, such as insects and spiders, have hard skeletons—called exoskeletons—on the outside of their bodies. Other invertebrates, such as worms and jellyfish, have soft, squishy bodies with no exoskeletons to protect them.

Here are three spiders that are closely related to tarantulas. Like all spiders, they are invertebrates.

Purseweb Spider

Funnel-Web Tarantula

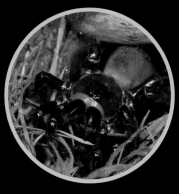

Trapdoor Spider

Glossary

backbone
(BAK-*bohn*)
a group of connected bones that run along the backs of some animals, such as dogs, cats, and fish; also called a spine

egg sac
(EG SAK)
the silk container that a female tarantula makes to protect her eggs

fangs (FANGZ)
long pointy teeth

spiders
(SPYE-durz)
small animals that have eight legs, two main body parts, and a hard covering called an exoskeleton

Index

Read More

Eckart, Edana. *Tarantula*. New York: Children's Press (2005).

Goldish, Meish. *Goliath Bird-Eating Tarantula*. New York: Bearport Publishing (2007).

Learn More Online

To learn more about tarantulas, visit
www.bearportpublishing.com/NoBackbone-Spiders

About the Author

Kathryn Camisa lives in New York City, where she works in children's publishing. When she isn't writing, she enjoys reading, listening to live music, and visiting museums.